Selah

Selah

Nora Gould

Brick Books

Library and Archives Canada Cataloguing in Publication

Gould, Nora, 1959–, author
        Selah / Nora Gould.

Poems.
Issued in print and electronic formats.
ISBN 978-1-77131-445-9 (paperback).—ISBN 978-1-77131-447-3 (pdf).
—ISBN 978-1-77131-446-6 (epub)

        I. Title.

PS8613.O914S45 2016   C811'.6   C2016-902774-0
                                               C2016-902775-9

We acknowledge the Canada Council for the Arts, the Government of Canada through the Canada Book Fund, and the Ontario Arts Council for their support of our publishing program.

The author photo was taken by E. Bronwen Gould.
The book is set in Sabon.
The cover image by Mr Doomits.
Design and layout by Marijke Friesen.
Printed and bound by Sunville Printco Inc.

Brick Books
431 Boler Road, Box 20081
London, Ontario N6K 4G6

www.brickbooks.ca

for Charl

Beside the piano he wouldn't play, his fingertips all slipped
into shallows between my ribs, drafted the longitude
of my midaxillary lines from the depths of my fossae
(*yes, my armpits, where I sweat*) down my torso.
He pressed as though to enter.

And this was a hug.

Breathe. There is air in the room.

In our bed, the window open
wide, night after night the hollow
tremolo of a snipe, winnowing.

Dusky blues, greens, shot with pearly light, yellows,
rosy pinks — twilight or dawn, nothing is decided. Goats,
grey, brindle, soft brown throats, underbellies flecked
with black. Unscissored beards, curved horns. An
undertow of semen.

The palette darker than I'd planned, all that
light to be sewn into nine-patches, a quilt
to layer with, or sleep under in another room.

Stitching the long seams across the breadth;
repeated kitty-corner, colour, slant-rhymed.
It is past time to question fabrics.

And that one goat, running — did I place both hands
on her head, turn her out into the wilderness?

What hadn't, might not happen, was already my fault.

Too unsettled
to know that place he loved
to buy coffee, a sweet, was just a block north

on our way home, he didn't talk
about our separate meetings, his new diagnosis —
frontotemporal dementia. We were both there

when the neurologist explained the medication,
how it should dampen the irritability, the drumming,
and his apathy. Six weeks until Bronwen's plea

convinced him to try it. Another month and he sang,
not often, but occasionally — *Splish splash I was taking a bath,*
and, *Seventy-six trombones bom de bom de bom.*

Waiting for my mother,

her death. Cradling between my palms a spruce
for this nascent windbreak, in prayer —
a psalm to Cheyne-Stokes, the northwest wind.

My cold knees saved by the up, walk, bend.
Zo, any message? I knelt to hold
the seedling upright — Zoë and her Pa ahead of me,

their shovels narrow-tongued — and pulled moist soil
from a perfect mound to gird the root.
A slight shake of her head. Two-handed, I formed

a lip of earth to hem in water, my frame steadied
with muscle. I stood, allowed the body its alignment,
an erectness through the shoulders; my breath even.

His shovel the metronome. Zoë worked
all the jobs in turn — dug the holes, hauled water,
planted. Her body a fluid column.

The third morning
Zoë opened her arms. Charl, a sound
in his throat. Earth, clay loam

in my hands, on my knees.
Bundles of spruce in burlap.

The creek high, snowmelt and spring rain.

Every overfilled pothole and slough —
ducks, grebes, shorebirds, coots.

The bee man moved his hives to higher ground.

Water around the great rocks in old buffalo wallows.

The more recently dropped — snippets of barbed wire,
fencing staples, that small pair of vise-grips,
draw pins, bushings and bearings — began a slow descent
countercurrent
to the rising of the long-believed-lost — blinkers and harness
buckles and thresher parts, seized and corroded.

The cow's neck chain with a solid metal disc stamped *16*
was unscathed among the rocks on the headland.

His kid's ball game convenient for the handover,
the Fish and Wildlife officer entrusted me with the kits.

White-tipped tails, ears unfolding, and grey woolliness
matted into their undercoats. A sharp stench.

Silent, they didn't need coaxing to feed. Some guy had shot
one parent, then the other because he saw them.

His dog dug out the young who were *too cute to kill.*
I scouted dens and phoned neighbours — a vixen in milk

and a kindly landowner all that were needed for fostering.
By the scruff, we dropped them down the burrow under Dana's shed.

That summer nine kits, four distinctly smaller, tussled in her yard.

Not a foreign language.

His lost words, delays to decipher, not speaking,
and the odd surprise — *Don't attach conditions.*
Tell me what to do and I will do it. Don't
make me figure things out.

I had said, *If you are warm enough, please*
turn down the heat.
We were in the car, looking ahead.

Cedar Waxwings devoured every petal from
the Siberian crab — the blossoms
already pollinated.

Refusing supper, he took a handful of almonds.
Silent. Awake.

In the morning he said, *I think*
you and the kids should decide together.

Not to avoid making my own decision.
It's because the doctor told me I can't see myself.

Maybe it's time to move on, give up driving, or maybe I should
try for a limited licence, then I could check the cows,

take them salt,
be useful.

Back from the cold room with chokecherry jelly —

What did you use to lift your soup?

That big spoon.

It has holes in it.

You know, I looked at that —
I didn't get my share of the broth.

How to reconcile
this
      with his grasp of the baler, the mesh
      of all those moving parts.

Bartlett pears ripe in the blue bowl,

the cast iron pan almost too heavy for my wrists,
I carried the frittata, set it on the trivet. I was a little drunk
on the throatiness of pullets rolling their *aws*. In their shed —

leaning, propped up — the sun passed through knotholes,
splintered wood, tongued dust motes, chaff,
into red-gold haze. The rhythm in my shoulders,
my torso, of pailing grain to cows, forking hay. The bedding

pulled in from the line. Mab, a pup then, sound asleep
on her blanket, her paws folded along her forelegs.
The south door opens directly into the kitchen
from outside. Our summer student, elegant, carried her quiet

grief — her mother dead these few months, her father
estranged. Charl followed her in — I saw that he had fallen
in love with her gentleness, her accent, her search
for words to humour him.

I didn't speak of this, didn't hear his denial,
until I had walked uphill towards the well,
the moon riding on the horse's withers. I should have waited
until I knew to let it go, but that was months later.

Even then I didn't fathom. I want to be forgiven.

I had to explain I'd made an appointment with the doctor.

He said, *Let me ride my horse forever.* He said,
If I'm going the wrong way turn me around, and

My horse will know the way home,

but nothing about the herd's direction, the neighbour's canola.

Conference call in preparation for
The Role of Working Memory in Guiding Step Trajectories.

*You understand that you've been asked to take part in this study
because you have been diagnosed with mild cognitive impairment.*

Yes

*All these questions are mandatory. This interview will take about
ten to fifteen minutes. Have you ever been diagnosed with mild
cognitive impairment?*

Please repeat the question.

Have you ever been diagnosed with mild cognitive impairment?

I have no idea what you are talking about.

Are you right- or left-handed?

I rope right, shoot left — I must be right-handed.

Charl, you write with your left hand.

I guess I do. I wonder why I ever started that.

Deliberate, I took myself outdoors, over
to the shed, layered mineral, salt, and dried
molasses, poured them back and forth. Three
five-gallon pails filled, I whistled
for Hazel and Mab to come with, to the cows.

Turning west off the pavement, I saw
on the sidehill the coyote, dead
several days now, up
shaking her brushy self.

A hank of alfalfa snagged
on the carcass.

He asked how much
spaghetti to cook. I stood beside him
peering into the pot. *First you need more water.*

Why? Right then I didn't (*couldn't?*) name this
harbinger.

Away from home,
and having Rob to talk to, bless him,
I recognized the turn, the new trajectory.

Through all this, his goodness. I was not
afraid.
        I wanted them gone, never mind
they were not loaded, rifles and shells
under separate key. His anger a breakthrough

bleed. Would I know to flee — what state of undress,
shoelessness, all that open ground,
whether
        I'd freeze, unaware I would again
        recognize his face, him, a good man.

He didn't see the overtime goal.
The morning was foggy.
He didn't follow what was said on the phone.
The potatoes weren't planted.
The armrest in the truck had come loose.

Four gates east, across the Watson Coulee to the field
where he had seeded cicer milkvetch.
Together we plucked stems,

clusters of furred seed pods,
fawn through dark brown,
barbed and susurrant with mourning.

On my writing table a fistful of sadness
beside the elephant ear begonia. It
came from my grandmother. Carrie.

Too sore even to walk the gravel when what I wanted was to run,
to have to concentrate on breath. Charl eyed my iliac crests,

assessed the symmetry of my pelvic girdle, studied my knees,
outlined my patellae in black ink, then said, *There's the problem,*

the left points ahead, the right outwards. He read me
healing instructions, checked the angles of my joints
with the photos, and laughed at my impatience with the clock.

The Rose-breasted Grosbeak three days
at the feeder; others, briefly. They
never stay.

Mother, *Grace*, sorry she never had children,
still knew the dog's name and shown pictures
of any hawk or owl said, *That's the bird I held.*

My sister took perfect care of her while I read
the updates, watched our farmhand, Georgie — his driving,
his coming back again for supper, 10:30 at night —
and Charl.

Writing about deer, that's maybe starting to work
but the direct references to *Mommy* —
pages of scribble. Last night I pieced more
nine-patch quilt blocks, but didn't finish
or iron any of them.

In strewn hay deer left their bodies'
imprints where they bedded in the lee — bales
five high, geese up there come spring. For days
we worked around the doe, her hay on bare
ground, her forelimbs disconnected

from her shoulders. Those photos of her
somehow overlapped with the ones my sister
made me promise to destroy. I loosed my hair

and untangled the knots beneath my braid.
Watering the plants, I turned sideways and
leaned back to pass the hoya's tendril.

Grace rallied.
I visited.
It was February.
I don't remember how the game started
or ended — likely she was tired. We played

catch with a bread tie
slid back and forth across polished wood.

I am writing to you from inside this,
my confusion. You will recognize yourself.
I don't know you, who you are, how to find you,
but I am aware I'm a person while I am with you.
Please forgive all the simple declarative sentences.

I am exhausted, lonely for you. Your refusal —
I didn't know I had asked, was it something
I said? body language? — told me what I carry,

how impossible it would be.
If you were to hold me, let me hold you —
these are two different things. Could
either of us allow either?

I miss him. That is
where I would be, where I am anyway,
not in his arms. This is not
guilt or impropriety.

Caffeine-tired, I can't sort this out
in a coffee shop
far enough from home to believe that
it is not true. Charl is himself

at the farm; he will still grab his chin
in mock consternation.
The shelf above the potato pail is
undisturbed. This is all my fault.

I will go home and Charl will be himself.
He is himself. That's the thing. He is.

I miss you. I miss
the possibility of you,
us.

I am in a hayfield, snow gathering
in folds and creases — my coat sleeves.

In the coulee,

last year's smaller-than-my-palm fine-grass-
nests sat about knee level in stout-thorned,

trunk-girdled bushes. A teasel idle
on the path having raised a green
nap through old grass. Crowfoot violets

on the sidehill. I came up thrashing at ants,
still wishing for a camera, images of Charl.

He had misplaced my mouth
that night he wanted me.
Even I couldn't discern this
as because of something I did or didn't do.

This was not long before the potato pails —
everything happened before or after,
windblown around markers themselves

eluvial. I set that night aside,
next to the candles
above the pegs where we hang our jeans.

I asked him to watch my bag; he said he would. I said,

If someone picked it up, you'd let them take it, because if
they picked it up, it must be theirs, in fact, if it were a woman

since the bag belongs to your wife, she must be your wife.
He laughed, said, *I'm not that far gone yet.*

His black cowboy hat reserving the seat beside him for me —
our only outing together. The first we'd spoken of this

in the months waiting for that initial neurology consult.
We had hoped we'd have an answer, some direction.

Yes. The night before the fire. More precisely, early
morning. The past needing to be documented, held.
We had watched ballet on television: *Love Lies
Bleeding*. Awake to the dance, he'd gone

to bed — sleep was quick — leaving open
jars of jam and peanut butter, the toaster plugged in.

A fire from a cigarette flicked out a vehicle window — this
was afterwards, early evening on the day of. Carryover
grass. Smoke. From the kitchen it looked imminent, not
miles south of the hill. Had it been dark, he'd have seen
his downswing scatter flame, his water-soaked
gunny sack quell it. In sparse stubble

the fire wasn't robust. Lost. All this after he rode
to move the heifers. His dapple grey, newly trained,
trotted up behind cattle, nipped at their asses. He said
he hadn't had a horse like that in forty years.

After the ballet, I had put the food away, let Hazel and Mab out,
then bathed by candlelight, and read. I still wonder —
was he aware beyond himself;

did this emanate from muscle;
if he tried, could try, to bid tenderness come;
or, on waking in the night, was he unfettered?

I told him he had stopped reading.
I should have told him sooner; I didn't know
he didn't know. He had stopped kissing me.

And how many years ago was that?

I took it personally. Suppose we were cooking together
and I kissed him (*is this like telling him he doesn't
kiss me?*), he would shrug, say,

Don't start something you can't finish.

Early evening over east, grouse lekking
on their ancestral ground stamped their feet
in courtship. A muffled booming, their necks

purple; tail up, head down. Leaving Charl
and Bronwen to their work, I was checking
cows, not bird watching, but stopped the truck

a ways away to use binoculars. Darkness
fell. Bronwen had said, *You shouldn't
say things that make him mad.* I could only

construe this as *you shouldn't speak to him.*

Alone, I could focus on what I saw — he had shoved
the taller potato pail in, forced the shelf up, set the shorter
one on the other side. Charl, who could measure distance
and size with his eye, his grasp of physics uncanny. In the quiet

of just us in the kitchen I asked him
about those pails, the shelf. He said,
I was in a hurry. I found no words. Perhaps

my eyebrows. He knew I knew, I could see
he knew and he knew that too and we didn't speak of it
all winter, Charl and I, on the farm.

November deep cold, a half-mile fence to rebuild
ready for the cows to swath-graze Waldron's.

Walk. Look back — the path a giant slalom, the oblivious
adjustment and readjustment of Everyman's trek. This is why

the scope is used to sight the fenceline.
He wielded the axe, dished each brace

to fit its post. I still believed I had seen the beginning in the fall,
that the bent shelf had been the index glitch. December, the herd home,

I wasn't vigilant — no grain in their ration.
I was blinkered from the decade gone — he had ratcheted back

his game of Clue (*he used to win*). He wrote fewer notes, then none,
but would still show a card, at times in error, and his own queries

seemed unrelated to his hand. Then he refused to play at all.
I failed him, misread his gist,

when he said, *I don't think like other people.*
He didn't (*couldn't?*) elaborate.

His anger, yelling, excuses given as reasons.
How he held himself apart, his look
that said *you bitch*. The way I accepted blame,

my busyness raising children,
and trying to manage work he shifted into
my responsibility. There is no excuse.

The momentum — the shovel heavy with April snow —
smashed my hand into the steel post. I finished the bunks,
cattle waiting for their feed. Truly, the pain came later.

In *his* appointment Georgie looked at his shoes and Charl agreed with
what I told the doctor. Forty-one years Georgie'd worked on this farm.

A memorial service for my mother. She'd given her body to science.
Charl with his papers for blood work and a referral for a CT scan.

Only when I said to Charl, *I want you to stay here with me,*
would he admit that Georgie should be in the Lodge.

He's been moved to long-term care.
My sister looked after Mother right to the end at home.

The doctor told me to get it in my head that I can't do that
for Charl. It's not the dying he says I won't be able to handle.

People keep telling me to make a plan.

I have an ectopic pregnancy
in my mediastinum,
a space-occupying lesion, acephalic,
that bulges into my throat, kicks
at my ventricles, obstructs breath.

I'm expecting a long gestation.

If I outlive him, when he dies
my grief will be stillborn.
I will grieve him
and my lack of grief.

Cattle rub on barbed wire fences, leave
thick dreads. Here in my east room,
a deep cup — woven horsehair, plant fibre,
four loops over slender branches and
an offshoot trussed to the body of the nest.

For the staged family photograph he bent to kiss me —
he did put his lips on mine,
his cowboy hat in front of my face.

I had put my hand on his shoulder, turned him to me
when he reached back, patted my forearm. He'd
lost the subtleness of — last month? Then the pressure

of his index finger on the nub of my bent elbow,
as though he sought *the lateral epicondyle*
of the humerus, origin of an extensor, a latch
to open both my arms.

I should have turned, faced the window where the sun
had set in the northwest, the shadow of the wayfaring bush
hovering with that snipe's falling
laughter. I swallowed. I will never have
a lover.

Enough.
Late, in April ditches, deer, the snow reluctant
under their slight heft —
delicate-hooved, they yearned toward earth
for purchase, to hoist themselves
                                        onward.

Bucks dragged their toes — furrows behind their hoofprints.

This is a time for happiness —

calm August evenings I head out at dusk,
pocket sweet crabs from the near tree (they ripen
first). Loosen the knot under my ribs. Wear
a hat, narrow brimmed, the straw the colour of clove

blossoms, the satin ribbon's dull sheen on the wider
matte-ribbed band, the bow demure, petals sewn flat, no tails.

Tuck in the pullets and old hens, close their doors against
coyotes and skunks. On the path east, veer into the pasture
a little south, a little downhill — enough to chill
the ankles. Shut in young hens roosting in their summer

quarters. Wander further, past spruce and caragana.
The slough is bedding down.
Go home. Detour back to the shed, the hen from beside

the black currants quiet under my arm. That fugitive warmth
between the plum bush and the hollyhocks is only there
while I am passing through — I mustn't succumb,
it's not enough to hold me.

Charl, flown, to fish
in northern Saskatchewan — my days
opened. Jeans, button-down shirt and
bandeau on the chair. Hazel supine, her legs
up the chesterfield back, Mab across the south
threshold. I, in a red shift for dreams, for sleep
to heal my carrot-harvest-shovel-foot, for
repose.

Last I nearly met you, vases, mason jars, my hands laden
with daisies, broken-stemmed (*how to set down
grief*). Photographed, quadrupled, white-petalled,
their shadows on the scrubbed-wood table
and both reflected in the dark window.

Only the mirrored tea in the exposure.
Now I half expected you, straight-backed
on the straight-backed chair beside my window.
My hand didn't (*couldn't?*) lift, fall,
on the blanket. Besides, you were
far away with your own sorrow.

I will write this later.

Unremarked, one fabric gave way
little by little. I dreamed about its reach,
how it mattered to the essence, the brio, of
this goat quilt I sleep under. I rummaged

deep in the drawer for that same colour
and eked out patches, pressed raw edges
underneath, hand-sewed them into place.
Combing through the quilt, I find more

deteriorating. Can I gather myself, be
diligent enough, to stave off
folding
         my cover onto the floor for the dogs?

Lidded glass bowls stacked three high.
He moved the uppermost left, onto

the two-quart measuring cup, picked up
the middle one, rattled it against the bowl

he'd just shifted, said,
Put the food away yourself.

Last year's grass through the snow —
Prairie's calligraphy.

The hooves, as if the leg still held them aligned.
The pedal bones tucked neatly inside, one middle
phalange gone, the other undisturbed. A strip of hide
fringed with hair, slightly askew. And right there in the
rough fescue, paired first phalanx bones, their four sesamoids
impossibly lined up. All the muscle and sinew stripped away.

His face closes. He folds shut.
Only his moustache recognizable.

Those pamphlets they give out say
there may be changes in intimacy.

My breath, short. My chest, his fulcrum.

I have time to love the irony of expressions,
to think words in my throat, repeat them
with the rhythm. How can I help it,
my larynx articulating each syllable.

I shouldn't have waited so long to push his shoulders, say,
I can't breathe.

Holding him to me, to my body, couldn't
erase our separateness.

And Charl? What about him, how he felt?
You — I am speaking to myself —

you can try to explore this. Don't pretend
you know. That ferocity. How it gripped him.

Barley streamed from the combine into the grain cart.
Our driving was synchronized until Matthew's blinked signal

for me to peel away, wait. The moon. I could see further,
the sloughs, with the tractor lights off. After the third load

I'd glance up from my rough draft to see if Farley
was back from the bin. Maybe Charl had sent tea.

Years ago, a letter from Maryanne —

No presage of the goat quilt.
And yet. They must have

bedded under it. *The fertility in your house*
rubbed off on us on Easter weekend.

The doe we carried from the sandy floor
of the machine shed — dry, light,
no fat to turn rancid. She'd have been rough-coated,
her breath sweet with ketones when she'd bedded
there out of the wind. Perhaps old hollyhock
blossoms, mugo pine needles in her belly.

The funniest part — Hazel knew before I did — isn't funny at all.
She would follow Charl to the porch, then while he put his boots on,
come back to the kitchen, stare at me, some days refuse
to go with him. I assumed it was her arthritis.

Neither Farley nor I know how or when
we both knew that we both knew
or what it was we thought we knew —

but with Zoë home to work on the farm
for the summer, we both knew she'd have to know
before she was around their Pa *and* machinery.

It was a Monday in May.
I phoned Matthew and Bronwen,
talked with Zoë in her bedroom.
The slightest pause. She said,

I saw without seeing.

My grandmother held the menses cloth in both her hands,
said, *Now why did I keep my rags?* We were cleaning the chest
in the closet that was the passageway on the second storey.

If Stewart had come home from the Great War, my mother
would have been older, someone else, and my father
not my father. I'd be a stranger to myself. There were two

staircases. The one from the front room with a north
window at the landing. In the kitchen, three straight steps,
a door, then the flight spiralled. I'd try to ascend

on the narrowest part. If I weren't me, I wouldn't have had
that house to love, the stovepipe through the bedroom. My
daughters and sons not threshing their memories for their Pa.

Heavy fog — the sun is pewter, a full moon.

Coyotes gleaned the ground and on their hind legs
pilfered apples and pears. Later, one returned now
and again to climb the southeast crab. I haven't seen
any of them in the bush by the kitchen window.

I look for my quickening — Charl on the path home,
his walk without its old intensity, his arm swing muted.

His body, as ever, windswept, like that smaller twin calf.

I stop with tea towel in hand. Magpie, a deep-lodged crab
exacting an open beak, ducks his head below his perch
to come up with a second. Both secure, he flies off.
I suppose he held his tongue just so.

Unable to talk him out of calling the service manager,
I found the number, dialed for him. Chided, he thrust

the receiver at me — *You have to get him to tear the header
down, find the problem. Good luck with that.*

Matthew hard at it, wrenches and sockets. When his Pa
overcame his apathy, they set the manual aside.

Tea in his left hand, right tapping the tabletop,
Charl was quietly furious through the search for the part,

a dealer who could get it faster. By the time it came in
he was chipper, suggested I go along for the drive —

he wanted me
                    to find the way.

Maryanne said, *It's called compensating.
Look back, probably years, recognize how
you've covered for him.*

He and Bronwen hang framed photographs
of his horses. He won't say if he wants the ochre

walls painted, wouldn't say which room
he'd move to, how he wanted the furniture

arranged. I'd told him that was the day — he would
have our bed, the ladderback chair. I kiss him,

his forehead, not knowing whether he is sleeping.
His window south for winter sun,

our two doors kitty-corner, ajar.

On the stone in the labyrinth, Mourning Cloak
butterflies in full June sun, conjoined —
the pattern on their wings a semicircle.

I couldn't fathom their stillness, the flux,
the continuum, of their coupling.

Moths settled
in my undergarments
on the clothesline.

The lotion cold, his flat-palmed slap prelude only
to his new laughter. No fugue bumped slowly
down my vertebrae, curved along my hip bone.

Elbows bent, unbuttoned
jacket slipped from my shoulders,
became patagium;
splayed fingers, primaries.
I soared — hollow bones breathed joy.
Nobody cares
                    what I'm doing
as long as the work is done.

Winter-bandaged hands, bulky
layers zippered shut. Thighs
pressed together — Prairie's
inland sea lapped my body.
Petrified wood from her erstwhile
trees next to the candles above
the pegs where I hang my jeans.

At his first appointment with the neurologist
the receptionist called me his *caregiver*.
I said, *No, his wife.*

Wearied by incremental mourning,
his withdrawal into
a culture of one,

I ache
for his songs,
his intricate drawings.

His Einstein hair, his six a.m. piano.

Reproachful, the dermatologist wrote myriad
prescriptions and sniped, *He shouldn't have taken oral
prednisone*, and, *Everyone knows the ears are part of
the scalp*. This was my fault. The light gone early

in late fall, Charl said, *Let my hair dry then
shave my head*. His ponytail was flaxen,
thick above the elastic, its scissored inner surface
velvety dark like his bristle. All that peripheral

vasodilation, he wore his new hat in the house.
Remote, he lifted his arms, rolled his shoulders
under my hands, turned, thrust his knees forward.
His hands, feet. A plateau, then plaques and guttate

lesions in resurgence. I don't know
what will happen, what will be lost — Hazel
missing her chesterfield.

Bells on the south kitchen door like when the kids were little.
Or through the basement, up the cement steps that in cold weather

are an extra fridge, as long as freezing doesn't matter. The shudder
of the house, where the air in that small place goes when the door

is shut hard, the way he does. I'm deafer now, have a deeper
exhaustion, a heavier sleep.

Will it be enough
to say *I didn't hear him?*

Bronwen read all this and brought up the unsolved
dilemma of her father driving on the farm,
but not for the telling here.

And she couldn't know about my rewriting
in the past tense.

She thinks I have not gotten across
her Pa's self-centredness, his selfishness.

To hell with us driving eleven miles home behind Farley
barefoot and wet in the tractor, minus forty and a wind,
his overalls solid in the truck box. The cows must have cracked
the slough ice. He wanted the chesterfield, the television.

His irritability. Everyone at table with him,
nauseous. I have to stay ahead, have things ready,
his pillow in its case before his bedtime.

The undercurrent of violence.
His volume.
His throwing whatever is at hand.
Bronwen cites incidents —

that day somehow nothing broke, not even his glasses,
and the first time he turned on Zoë (*I couldn't stop him*).
Her whole body trembled. Matthew said,
He was like that with me this morning.

His years of gradual change from himself, to *this*, became
unmuddied — I hadn't always been at fault.

He wouldn't hold my hand or look at me after
the appointment. At home he asked, *Am I allowed
to know my diagnosis?*

Inlaid on the crest of Campbell Hill —

the left foreleg with its paw grounded
is the weight-bearing strut,

the body's pivot, the lead. Fox, loping
in an aureole of gravel.

A new constellation, the right ear
cocked due north.

Opening Phrases

Acknowledgements and Notes

My gratitude to

the editors of *Contemporary Verse 2*, *Eighteen Bridges*, and *PRISM international* where excerpts from *Selah*, in earlier versions, appeared

The Alberta Foundation for the Arts
The Banff Centre
Sage Hill
St. Peter's College

Brick Books

Kimmy Beach
Phil Hall
Don McKay
Erin Rubert
Rob Taylor
Seán Virgo

and

as always, my family.

—

Yes, I know, door alarms.

Nora Gould writes from east central Alberta where she ranches with her family. Her previous poetry collection, *I see my love more clearly from a distance*, was published by Brick Books in 2012.